WHEN THE ORDINARY WON'T DO!

How ordinary people can experience the extraordinary in life

L.A. Kimo Richardson

Foreword by Bishop George Searight

Copyright © 2007 by L.A. Kimo Richardson

WHEN THE ORDINARY WON'T DO!
by L.A. Kimo Richardson

Printed in the United States of America

ISBN 978-1-60266-062-5

All rights reserved under International Copyright Law. The author guarantees all contents are original and do not infringe upon the legal rights of any other person or work. Contents and/or cover may not be reproduced in whole or in part in any form without the expressed written consent of the Author. The views expressed in this book are not necessarily those of the publisher.

Unless otherwise indicated, all Scripture quotations are taken from the King James Version of the Bible.

www.xulonpress.com

ACKNOWLEDGEMENTS:

There are so many people that I could thank for their assistance in writing this book. Thank you to Diane Tucker, Neena Brown, Cynthia Pierre, and Janaka Bowman for all your assistance in helping me to proofread and clarify the contents of this book. I would also like to say thank you to all the individuals that made contributions to the publishing of this book, you'll never know how much your vote of confidence means to me. A special thank you to Henry Uzochukwu, Shaneika Nelson, and Edmund Odoi for your special contributions to the publishing of this book, I will be eternally grateful. Finally, I would like to say thank you to my family for allowing me to monopolize the computer so that I could type, re-type, and do that process all over again.

TABLE OF CONTENTS:

FOREWORD

I am sure that you have heard at one time or another that it is the will of God that you live a consecrated life. If I may infringe upon you for one moment, what does the word consecration mean to you? I am sure that if you look up the word consecration in the dictionary, you will find that it gives the meaning "to set apart". When you think about it, the mere fact that you attend church every week "sets you apart" from someone who does not attend church. So what is the real importance of living a consecrated life? Let me put it this way…What is the importance of living a lifestyle of consecration?

Easton's Bible Dictionary defines the word consecration as "*the devoting or setting apart of anything to the worship or service of God*". This definition gives clarity to God's design and will for your life. The truth is that it is easy to live a life that is "set apart". As I pointed out earlier, you can be set apart from those who do not attend church services. Furthermore, demographics such as race, ethnicity, income, age, and sex can set you apart from others.

However, I want to bring your focus to the latter part of that definition that says the devoting or setting apart *of anything to the worship or service of God*—which is the will of God for your life.

It is clear that you have been chosen to worship and serve God in every area of your life. In 1 Peter 2:9-10 it says:

> *"But you are not like that, for you are a chosen people. You are a kingdom of priests, God's holy nation, his very own possession. This is so you can show others the goodness of God, for he called you out of the darkness into his wonderful light. Once you were not a people; now you are the people of God. Once you received none of God's mercy; now you have received his mercy."*

Once you accepted Christ as your savior, you became apart of the people of God because it is the will of God that none should perish. It is His will that you are apart of the kingdom order and serve as a priest. In Revelation 1:6 you will see that when Christ died he made "*us his Kingdom and his priests who serve before God his Father*". Although sin made you unworthy to receive the blessings of God, Christ's blood covered you and made you worthy and acceptable unto God—making you a priest.

The call of the priest is not easy. You may want to name it and claim it, without being obedient to the word of God. This is impossible! Your obedience qualifies you for the blessings of the Kingdom. If you look at 1 Peter 2:8, you will see that if you live a life beneath your priestly call that it is because you were disobedient to God's Word. In 1 Peter 2:8 it says, *"They stumble because they do not listen to God's word or obey it."* God has given you everything that you need in His Word for you to live a consecrated life.

In this book, my spiritual son, Kimo Richardson, teaches that consecration trains you to operate in the kingdom of God. You will also learn that true consecration takes the focus off of your problems and places the focus on God.

I am honored to be apart of history in Kimo's life. For Kimo, this book becomes a marker or stone of the awesome thing God is going to do in and through him. God is going to use him mightily as he ministers and builds true disciples of Jesus Christ. It is my desire that you will be blessed beyond measure as you truly begin to live out your priestly call.

Bishop George C Searight
Senior Pastor, Abundant Life Family Worship
Church—New Brunswick, NJ

INTRODUCTION

It would be wonderful if I could say that I was on the mountaintop seeking the Lord for forty days and nights, when the Lord took His finger and began to inscribe this message of extraordinary living on the pages of my yellow legal notepad, but that wasn't the case. I just happened to be spending some time with the Lord one evening in late November of 2004 with a growing hunger for something different, but not really knowing what exactly would bring about that difference in my life.

As I continued my time with the Lord I began to flip through my bible on the way to begin a study of Genesis chapter one when I happened upon the sixth chapter of the book of Numbers and the wonderful message it contained. As I read the chapter, I thought to myself "hmmm…this is interesting there must be something more to this scripture than I can see right now," and with that thought began a wonderful journey of seeking the extraordinary hand of God to be in operation in my life. The more time that I spent with this message I began to think that maybe someone else would benefit from it so I put the precepts that I discovered in book form.

The secret that I discovered in Numbers six really isn't a secret at all it is all throughout the scriptures, but it has been shrouded in religiosity. The secret is simply this, the extraordinary is attainable for all of us, but there is a process associated with it. Consecration is that process. So many times when we hear the message of extraordinary living, it is presented as five simple steps that if you do these five things you will automatically step into greatness. The person presenting the message portrays himself as an expert on the topic who deserves to be listened to.

The truth is that most of us, including the experts, embark upon the journey to the extraordinary because we are facing an emotional or circumstantial crisis that we often are at a loss to describe and feel ill-equipped to handle. While there are no doubt persons that have achieved great feats in life, and there are clear steps to seeing the extraordinary occur in your life this book and author take a slightly different angle in presenting this message to you.

Instead of being your expert on the subject I choose to be your companion, we'll let the Word of God be the expert. Rather than presenting five steps to greatness we'll look at the entire process of seeking the extraordinary so that we can understand what is required of us and what is given to us in each dimension of the process. At each chapter I leave you with an extraordinary instruction, a specific action that you can take that will further you on your journey to activate the precepts within the correlating chapter.

I have placed my thoughts and reflections about my continuing journey to the extraordinary online at www.kimorichardson.com, and I invite you to share your reflections and reactions to the extraordinary instructions in the online forum as well. So if you are willing join me in the journey, I'll see you at the first chapter and then on the website.

CHAPTER 1:

AN UNDISCOVERED REVELATION

"Then the LORD spoke to Moses, saying, "Speak to the children of Israel, and say to them: 'When either a man or woman consecrates an offering to take the vow of a Nazarite, to separate himself to the LORD" *(Numbers 6:1-2)*

When you hear the word consecration, what image does it trigger in your mind? Take a moment, think about it. Do you envision someone fasting and praying for a long period of time? Do you think of someone who is older or younger? How does a consecrated person dress? How does the conse-crated person relate to the rest of the world; Are they holier-than-thou, or are they so merciful that they become pushovers? Why are people consecrated? Is it to take a special position in the church or to live an extraordinary life in the world?

It is important that you take the time to consider these questions because the pre-constructed image that you have in your mind about what the consecrated person is like will determine if you will ever become one. We talk a good game in the church when it comes to consecration but I really don't think that we understand it. Consecration is not just for the few "spiritual people" in the church, nor is it simply an event to be participated in by fasting at the beginning of the year or during the Lenten Season. The benefits that it positions the believer for are unmatched by any other activity the believer can ever undertake.

Spiritual Techniques

Consecration is an undiscovered revelation in the body of Christ. It is undiscovered because godliness has been reduced into various spiritual methodologies and techniques that when followed are thought to lead to spiritual success. In the first method, the Christian hides behind expensive cars, fine clothing, and rehearsed reactions to intellectually based preaching or emotionally based worship experiences. In the second method, the Christian portrays himself as a suffering serf simply trying to maintain in this life while placing his hope in the life to come.

In the first technique the believer covers himself up with things that create the image of success in order to hide his true nakedness. In the second technique the believer strips himself of what he deems to be worldly success, but not because he is actually humble. He emphasizes his humanity so that no one can ever expect divine authority and power to be expressed through him. By this action he makes God responsible for what he himself should control.

A Different Kind of Believer

For many Christians these formulas for successful Christian living suffice. They suffice because the believers that employ them are able to rationalize and excuse the tragedies they face in life. So long as they are able to do so they never see the need to experience the extraordinary hand of God in their lives. Crisis for most believers, whether experienced by the believer personally or by extension in the lives of those around them, will trigger either of the two responses noted above, but every so often the crises of life happen to a different kind of believer. When this believer encounters personal and public crises causing their world and the world of those to whom they have been assigned to spin out of control they feel the utter helplessness of being able to do nothing, however, a new desire is also triggered within them, a desire to see the extraordinary.

When this new desire registers in their minds they begin to question why they can't have an impact on the events that happen in their world. They ask themselves: How can I better control the desires of my flesh? How can I confront the situations and circumstances that I see in the lives of others and see those situations changed for the glory of God? Crisis has exposed them to just how mundane their lives are and dares them to believe that as a Christian they are positioned in this world for far more.

How can the Christian in this situation access more? He can trust in a God that is bigger than him and he can reach for a power that is greater than his to deal with the crises that he will face in this world. When crisis causes the Christian to come to the end of himself it is at this point that consecration begins.

True consecration is always born out of the crisis of our humanity. It is born in our hearts when we realize that we can never be the fullness of who we desire to be without tapping into God's power. Sanctification is developed when we understand that the situations we face in our lives and the mandate that God has placed over our lives are so big, that they will require more than we can ever muster in our own strength. They require extra above our ordinary and God is the only source of that extra. True consecration takes the focus off of us and puts the focus on to God and on to His ways.

A Different Pattern

God knowing that regenerated men would want to rise above the crises of this sin-sick world to the initial mandate of dominion that He declared over us in Genesis 1:28 left an illustration in His word so that we would know the way to do it. God told Moses in Numbers the sixth chapter to speak to the children of Israel—all the children of Israel; the old and the young, the male and the female, the rich and the not-so-rich and describe to them His extraordinary plan for their lives. Moses was to inform the people that if they ever came to a crossroads in their lives where they knew that they needed the hand of God to be operative in their lives in an extraordinary way they should vow the vow of the Nazarite.

Nazarite means "consecrated one" (Blue Letter Bible). Connected to the meaning of this word is the experience of a lifetime. When Numbers 6:2 talks about a man or a woman consecrating an offering when they vow the vow of the Nazarite, the word consecrate in the Hebrew language paints an unbelievable picture of possibility and hope. To consecrate in Numbers 6:2 means to do something extraordinary, surpassing, or to be separate by a distinguishing action (Blue Letter Bible). Consecration is an extraordinary action that evokes an extraordinary reaction from God.

All throughout the Old and New Testaments we see a pattern begin to arise; Samson was a Nazarite, John the Baptist was a Nazarite, Paul the Apostle was a Nazarite. Each of these men encountered crises in their lives that made it clear to them that they needed extra above the ordinary to deal with the situations that they were facing. They determined in their hearts that they would not leave the extraordinary to a special few, but that they too in their life could experience the hand of God.

Whenever we look at consecration in the Old Testament no matter who was being consecrated there was always a list of perquisites that had to be fulfilled before that person could be consecrated. To be consecrated a priest you had to be from the line of Aaron without any physical deformities. To serve as a Levite you had to be from the family of Levi. To be consecrated a king you had to be from the line of

David. Many of those anointed prophets in the Old Testament were also priests and Levites. In other words you always had to qualify in some way in order to be used in those capacities, but in Numbers 6 we find that God begins to speak to us about a different kind of consecration altogether–The consecration of the ordinary man to an extraordinary life, the life of a Nazarite.

When the ordinary won't do

When everything is normal or at least is perceived to be normal the ordinary will do. When you can manipulate a situation by your own intervention the ordinary will do, but when you, your family, your church, or your nation are facing a crisis the ordinary just won't do, you need extra! Samson needed extra to deliver Israel; you may need extra to deliver your son or your daughter. John needed extra to prepare the way for the Lord's coming; you may need extra to prepare the way for God's visitation on your ministry or your marriage. What you need God to do extra in I don't know, but if ever we were in need of believers that are a cut above the norm with a supernatural anointing in every arena of life, it is now!

Consecration is the Kingdom key to seeing the hand of God in your life. It is God's training tool whereby we are trained to operate in His Kingdom. Consecration is the only legitimate way to expect the extraordinary in the Kingdom of God. Are you ready for extra?

Extraordinary Instruction:

1. Take out a piece of paper and a pen and write down what words or thoughts come to mind when you hear the word consecrate or consecration.

Journaling the Journey

**Consider sharing your thoughts and reflections
on www.kimorichardson.com.**

CHAPTER 2:

THE LAW OF THE EXTRAORDINARY

Then the LORD spoke to Moses, saying, "Speak to the children of Israel, and say to them: 'When either a man or woman consecrates an offering to take the vow of a Nazarite, to separate himself to the LORD" *(Numbers 6:1-2)*

Consecration is not simply one step among many different steps that we must traverse on our way to seeing the extraordinary hand of God in our lives, it is the single most important step that we must undertake. God is a God of law and order; the world spiritually and naturally is orchestrated according to divine law. When we consecrate we are engaging the law of the extraordinary. Consider that for a moment, seeing the extraordinary is a legal action not one based on currying favors or manipulating God. It is caused by recognizing the pattern of God and then doing what He would have you do.

"The fear of the Lord is the beginning of wisdom", in other words respect for the pattern of the Lord is the evidence that you are truly wise and have understanding (Proverbs 1:7). God desires the extraordinary so much in your life that He has laid out the pattern in His word so that you can activate it in your life. He is no respecter of persons, Moses and Elijah are not the only ones to whom the extraordinary has been availed, you too can have it if you are willing to embrace your legal responsibility.

When we consecrate according to Numbers 6:2, we begin to take on that responsibility. We engage ourselves in the kind of life that causes us to be great and surpassing because we have separated ourselves by a distinguishing action. Holiness is what distinguishes us. Holiness is our legal responsibility in the Kingdom of God.

A Holy Set-Up

Holiness is often portrayed as our difference from others in the world, but really it is the difference of our former selves to our present selves. Even the most sainted individual needs to constantly distinguish his new nature from his old nature. If we were truly honest with ourselves we would admit that we are our own worst enemy when it comes to really living a distinguished life. It can be so easy at times to continue being who we were in sin instead of letting Christ make us who we are in Him.

The type of consecration exhibited in the life of the Nazarite deliberately set him or her up for extraordinary living. When we properly understand the plan of God for our lives we come to understand that the extraordinary is supposed to be ordinary in our lives. We must begin to allow the Lord to broaden our personal vision by submitting to the leadership of the Holy Ghost so that we each can see the great things that have been freely given to us (1. Cor. 2:12).

When we understand that God has more in store for our lives than we presently perceive it becomes all the more clear why He would make extraordinary living a Kingdom law to be engaged rather than an automatic perk of being in the Kingdom. If it were a perk it would be exploited, but as a law you must count up the cost and decide whether or not you are able to bear it. You must decide to want the more of God, extra given to you means extra is required of you (Luk. 12:48).

A Distinguished Lifestyle

You would think that a lifestyle that is designed to bring out the extraordinary in an individual would be filled with extra special rituals, high-maintenance habits, and unreasonable legalistic obligations, but truthfully consecration is basically a re-emphasis of the most fundamental elements of dedicated living. Consecration in its purest form is total life pursuit of a single focus. The issue is that most believers, in times past and in times present, are unwilling to wholeheartedly commit themselves to and focus their lives for greatness.

The truth is that when you become extraordinary you become distinguished and noticeable and there is a unique burden that you must now bear, but most are unwilling to bear it. Be encouraged though, when you consecrate yourself to the will of God the promise of God is sure, "the yoke will be easy and the burden will be light" (Matt. 11:30). The burden of extraordinary living is consecration. Will you bear it?

On the Advance

God assists us in bearing the burden of the greatness every minute, hour, and day of our lives. As we sow our chronos—minute by minute time into consecrating ourselves to the Lord we reap God's karios time–God's right now moment of being endued with power. What is that power? The unique ability that God grants the Nazarite is the ability to consecrate things. When we consecrate a thing we set it aside for a particular use or service. You engage in consecration everyday of your life; you consecrate your toothbrush for brushing your teeth, your forks for eating, and your cups for drinking.

As we become persons whose lives are characterized by being focused on the Lord, God then grants us the ability to consecrate everything we face in life as being useful and purposeful. We are able to do this because we have been vested with spiritual authority. The Nazarite is legally empowered to place under God's authority what is within him, what is upon him, and what is around him.

In every other type of consecration in Scriptures the person consecrated was consecrated by someone else, after all, no man was supposed to "take honor unto himself" (Hbr. 5:4). The consecration of a Nazarite is the only exception in the Scriptures, in this type of consecration God prepares you to be a consecrator.

The power to consecrate things is not new to mankind in fact Adam was consecrating things even in the Garden of Eden. The Scripture declares that all the animals that God created were brought to Adam to see what he would call them, and whatever Adam called them was what they were named (Gen. 2:19). The power to grant to the creatures their names reflected the authority to define what those creatures would be. Adam did not create the creatures but he could determine his relationship with them.

The same authority is granted to each of us as we focus our lives on the Lord. There is no situation that you should meet as you live the consecrated life that ought to dictate to you who you will be, but you should always declare to it what it shall be with the confidence that Heaven is backing you up.

Does this sound like too much? Let's consider what Jesus has to say on the subject "If ye abide in me and my words abide in you, you shall ask what you will and it shall be done for you" (John 15:7). God left the power of consecration in Adam's hands, Jesus left the power of consecration in the hands of His earliest disciples the question we must ask ourselves is why isn't it in ours?

We have lost the ability in the church to conse-crate things outside of ourselves because we will not consecrate ourselves. Think about it, how can we put things outside of ourselves under God's control if we will not put ourselves under God's control? Most believers if they were to be truthful would have to admit that they and the situations around them are indeed out of control. Our flesh is out of control, our finances are out of control, and our families are out of control. This lack of control is further evidenced by our constant retreat from areas that we should be advancing in. Jesus said that the very gates of Hell would not prevail against us, so why are we always on the run in our homes, in our churches, and in our nations (Matt. 16:18)?

Are you tired of retreating? Do you need extra to advance? God is willing to give you the extra you need, but He requires a decision from you, will you vow the vow of the Nazarite? Will you engage the principle law of the extraordinary in the Kingdom of God?

A Vow to make: Decide and Declare

When we vow the vow of the Nazarite God then begins to direct us into what consecration for the extraordinary means for our daily lives. At the moment that you decide to become a consecrated man or woman of God you must also in that very moment begin to ask the Lord, what kind of seed must I sow in order to see the mighty works of God? The Nazarite had to decide the offering that he would give the Lord at the very moment he vowed the vow of the Nazarite. Yes, consecration requires an offering nearly every type of consecration recorded in the Old Testament had coupled with it a consecration offering. You must consider carefully what you will give to your God.

What is God supposed to multiply in your life? You must allow God to paint the picture of the end result that He has for your life and you must be willing to offer that future to the Lord. Don't worry, that picture will connect with the desires of your heart, but it will do so at levels and at depths that you are not even conscious of because God knows you even better than you know yourself.

In response to the depth of desire that some Old Testament and New Testament Nazarites discovered, some submitted the entirety of their lives to being prepared for their calling. The future that they saw was just that big. Others consecrated for a period of time in preparation for a special work of service. The truth is we will all experience different crises in our lives and in the area that God has assigned us to and the length of time that it takes for one to prepare to meet the challenge in an extraordinary way it may not take for another.

For some of us, because God knows the level of crisis that we will face in our lives He has planted a seed of wisdom in those that raised us so that they would be able to raise us in the principles of consecration whether they fully recognized what they were doing and regardless of whether we appreciated it. This is what He did for Samson, and for John the Baptist, as a matter of fact, there was an entire clan in Old Testament Israel whose patriarch instructed them in the ways of the Nazarite and instituted elements of it as a law for all generations to follow (Jer. 35:6).

Even with all this it still remains up to each one of us to actively pursue extraordinary living by integrating the core principles of the consecrated life into our daily lives.

Whatever depth of crisis you are preparing yourself to face getting the extra will mean giving the extra. "To him who has more will be given" the Scripture says, but if you don't even have a vision of the extraordinary how can you ever receive it (Matt. 13:12)? The extraordinary results you want to achieve start with you opening your mouth and declaring to God the thing that you will offer to Him. You may not see the whole picture yet, but say what you see and God will honor it. We consecrate with the end in mind which is being able to give God an acceptable offering. Consecration benefits you, but is focused on God's will being done in your life. Offer to God that area of your life that is out of control that area that you want to see Him make an extraordinary move in, it is in that very area that God will begin to do the extraordinary in your life.

So I say, so I do! The Process Begins

Now that you have settled in your mind that the ordinary will not do and you have devoted to God those particular areas of your life and calling that you want to see Him do the extraordinary in you may be asking yourself is that all that is needed? No, God has so much more! He intends to put your faith in to action. Not only do you have a vow to make according to Numbers 6, but there is also a process that you must internalize and fulfill.

When we ask God for the extraordinary he invites us to take a journey deeper and deeper into His Kingdom. He teaches us how to engage the law of the greatness so that we can expect results. God's goal in our lives is not just for us to consecrate a singular offering to Him but He intends to also consecrate the entirety of who we are so that we can be agents of the extraordinary and not just have an extraordinary experience once or twice in our lives.

As we have a tri-dimensional relationship with God, that being God-in-us, God-on-us, and God-with-us, so consecration is a tri-dimensional process, in each dimension we internalize a little extra above that which is ordinary. As we come to understand the process of consecration we will understand what God expects us to do in order to fulfill the vow that we have made to Him as well as how God now empowers us to live an extraordinary life. Let's go deeper and explore this process in depth.

Extraordinary Instruction:

1. Picture [As vividly as you can] what the extraordinary hand of God would look like in your life. Write this down, post it in a prominent place, and begin to declare daily this extraordinary expression of God's presence to be a reality in your life.

Journaling the Journey

**Consider sharing your thoughts and reflections
on www.kimorichardson.com.**

CHAPTER 3:

THE EXTRAORDINARY INSIDE

"He shall separate himself from wine and similar drink; he shall drink neither vinegar made from wine nor vinegar made from similar drink; neither shall he drink any grape juice, nor eat any fresh grapes or raisins. All the days of his separation he shall eat nothing that is produced by the grapevine, from seed to skin." *(Number 6:3)*

The first thing that God instructed the Nazarite to do as a part of his consecration was to cease from consuming anything that was produced by the grapevine from seed to skin. God in his infinite wisdom chose to represent our consecration of the inward man by directing us to abstain from the grapevine in all forms.

Why abstain from the grapevine? The grapevine in scripture, and particularly wine—the product of the grapevine is used to represent that which predisposes one to sin. While the wine is not sin, the more it is ingested the more likely it becomes that you will sin. We see this illustrated even in the book of Genesis, where Noah was concerned.

In Genesis 9:21 the Scripture records Noah being so drunk that he lay unconscious and shamefully uncovered in his tent. This act was not only a sin for Noah but it also brought out sin in his family line through the acts of his son Ham. Also in the book of Revelation we see that the harlot is accused of making the nations drunk with the wine of her fornication (Revelation 17:2). Along with these texts there are plenty of other exemplifications in the Scripture that make wine analogous to sin.

Red Wine: The nature of sin

Let's consider the nature of sin for a moment, for that we will need to turn to Genesis 3:1-5.

> "Now the serpent was more cunning than any beast of the field which the Lord God had made. And he said to the woman, "Has God indeed said, 'You shall not eat of every tree of the garden?" And the woman said to the serpent, "We may eat the fruit of the trees of the garden; but of the fruit of the tree which is in the midst of the garden, God has said 'You shall not eat it, nor shall you touch it, lest you die.'" Then the serpent said to the woman, "You will not surely die. For God knows that in the day you eat of it your eyes will be

opened and you will be like God, knowing good and evil." *(Genesis 3:1-5)*

If there is anything that we should learn from this Genesis story it is what the nature of sin is. Sin is any attempt to know both good and evil at the same time, this is why the tree in the midst of the Garden is called the tree of the knowledge of good and evil. When Genesis 3:5 says that Adam and Eve would be "like God, knowing good and evil" in the original language knowing (yada) is a Hebrew word that connotes having an experiential acquaintance with something (Blue Letter Bible). As you partook of this fruit you would experience not just learn intellectually about good and evil.

We are trapped by most sins because a good and valid desire that we have in our lives is hooked up with an evil motive or manner of expressing that desire. We are often caught in sin unawares because we become blind to the fact that many of the things we are seeking after are both good and evil simultaneously.

Take a closer look at the Genesis 3 story and you will soon discover a simple fact; Eve drank the wine that the serpent was serving long before she ever ate the fruit he was offering. As she was so are we, we are blinded to the evil hidden in the good because we are made drunk and predisposed to mixing the two together.

Drunken Desire

We are all born drunk. It is as the psalmist said "Behold, I was shapen in iniquity; and in sin did my mother conceive me" (Psalms 51:5). We are born predisposed and as we continue to live we are further intoxicated. Temptation is the Enemy's attempt to intoxicate our lives. We are intoxicated by three things doubts, lusts, and pride. It is as the Scripture says "all that is in the world [is] the lust of the flesh, the lust of the eyes, and the pride of life" (1 John 2:16).

The lust of the flesh goes into operation when the five senses and the needs of the body begin to control our lives; we live to eat, or to have sex, etc... The lust of the eyes is not so much physical sight as it is perception, it is when we begin to be held captive and driven by our thoughts, desires, and emotions instead of them being captive to us. As for the pride of life, there is a certain pride humans experience in living outside of right relationship with God. Whether we fully understand it or not, we come to believe that because we have lived without His presence in our lives that He is not real or we do not need Him to live successfully.

As we look at Adam and Eve's case, the fruit appealed to their basic need for food—the lust of the flesh, the fruit was a source of pleasure because it was desirable to look at—the lust of the eyes, and the fruit gave them an intellectual advantage—the pride of life (Genesis 3:6). None of these desires are in and of themselves sinful, but the manner in which they went about fulfilling those desires was in direct disobedience to the command of God, a fact that they

38

lost sight of through drinking the wine of temptation that the devil served them.

You may be asking yourself, why would Adam and Eve disobey the command of God when they so intimately experienced His love and His presence? They did it because they were led to doubt Him. At the heart of every temptation is the enemy's attempt to make us doubt that God has an adequate means of fulfilling the needs and desires of our lives, and most importantly that He is our chief need and should be our chief desire.

When we sin, we fail to remember that God is the One who gave us our desires and that we were created to be like Him; our being like Him includes desiring like Him (Gen. 1:26). For every desire that we have God has already created a way for that desire to be met. Think about the last time that you have been in serious doubt and frustration. Did you tend to do things and say things that you never thought that you would? Did you end up sinning? What happened there? Doubt predisposed you to sin–it made you drunk, sin seemed like the best solution.

Doubt is the gateway into lust and into pride. When we doubt God's provision we create a thirst in our lives. The longer we thirst the more intense the thirst becomes. Our God-given desires then become uncontrolled lusts that we will use ungodly means to fulfill. When that lust is allowed to linger long enough it eventually creates a new taste in our mouths. We then become addicted to the new taste. The sin that we now commit is less about fulfilling the original desire that we started with and more about servicing our addiction. We often "transgress by wine" (Hab. 2:5) because we add "drunkenness to thirst" (Deut 29:19). At first we seek to quench our thirst but it soon becomes an addictive habit of which we are no longer in control.

Pleasurable Pain

When we understand that our desires which go unmet in the way that God intends for them to be met create an addictive thirst in our lives, we can more clearly understand why the Scripture compares temptation to wine. Proverbs 24:31-32 says,

> "Do not look on the wine when it is red, when it sparkles in the cup, when it swirls around smoothly; at last it bites like a serpent, and stings like a viper."

Wine is by its nature addicting. Wine has a strong and potentially intoxicating influence that can have two side-effects in the consumer simultaneously, it produces pleasure and it produces pain, or better yet it produces pleasurable pain and painful pleasure. Wine relaxes you, it calms your nerves but it also makes you do what you don't want to do. It leaves you open to the manipulation of others. Wine appears delightful and freeing but it is truly a serpent in the end.

Even Jesus faced the serpentine nature of the cup of sin when He declared that He thirsted on the cross. In response to Christ's declared need they offered Him sour wine to numb the pain of crucifixion. It wasn't until Jesus tasted the sour wine on the cross and rejected it that He gave up His spirit and He died (John 19:28-29). I believe that His drinking the wine represents the point in the crucifixion at which He became sin. The sour wine that was supposed to take away the pain of crucifixion became the venom that filled His body with sin.

The Effect of Sin

As the sour wine had an effect on Jesus, so sin has an effect on our lives. That effect can be clearly understood when we examine the impact that natural wine has on the physical body. When we drink alcoholic beverages, experts tell us that a few things happen; we lose our ability to make accurate judgments, our motor skills are diminished, and we risk death by alcohol poisoning ("Effects of Alcohol"). As in the natural so in the spiritual, we can be so filled with wine that we lose our wisdom, the ability to control our desires, and we risk death of the destiny that God has in store for our lives.

You may be saying, well I do not think that I am drunk with sin. By what standard are you judging? You may not be committing the act of sin, but you just as surely may not be walking out the fullness of God's purpose in your life. When we look at God's directive to the Nazarite we see that He instructed the Nazarite to abstain from the fruit of the vine from skin to seed. This note is very important. You may not be drunk with wine but you still help yourself to a grape every now and again. What you don't realize is that every sip you take and every grape you eat limits your ability to do the will of God and increases the

41

likelihood that you will commit an act of sin. This is why you keep on hitting ordinary although you are aiming for the extraordinary.

Many of us are more affected by sin and temptation to sin than we realize. You may be in a weakened state right now because weeks ago you started eating grapes and drinking grape juice. You convinced yourself that since it was not technically a sin and that you would be able to handle it. What you are not realizing is that the remnants of these products of the vine have now settled in your life and are fermenting into wine. Those doubts, desires, thoughts, and emotions that the enemy has tempted you with and you have accepted into your life are slowly intoxicating you.

Temptation to sin affects us in ways that we cannot register because we either do not understand it, or are not willing to acknowledge the fact that it is there. What's more, not only do we underestimate the power that sin can have on our lives, (and if we are to be really true to the Scriptures the effect it has on your friends and family) we also underestimate the power that the remembrance of sin can have in our life. When we meditate on sin we commit the act over and over again in our minds, and it makes us just as drunk as if we had actually been doing the sin all along. We can think about something so long that it becomes a part of who we are. We actually become it to the point that we cannot see ourselves being anything else.

A Life Diminished

The presence of sin and unresolved temptation in our lives reduces our ability to judge what is right from what is wrong. It reduces our ability to differentiate God from the world. Through sin we lose our wisdom, and are relegated to impulse. Wisdom is simply the ability to apply knowledge. The Bible calls the wisdom of this world, "earthly, sensual, and demonic" (James 3:15). The wisdom of this world is based on the impulses of the flesh. When we are intoxicated with sin, the only way that we know how to apply knowledge is in an earthly, sensual, and demonic way. To put it a little more bluntly sin has a dumbing effect on our lives, we are wise unto ourselves, but never beyond ourselves.

Not only is our wisdom diminished through sin and the memory of sin, our ability to act with skill is also lessened. When a person is severely drunk they lose the ability to use their motor skills, they can no longer function with accuracy and precision in the basic functions of life. Have you ever noticed that drunken persons can't even walk straight, an activity that they have engaged in with skill every day of their sober life? With that in mind the application beyond the effects of wine on the body to the effects of sin on the entirety of our lives becomes clearer. Through sin we lose the ability to coordinate our life's activities in the direction of our life's purpose.

We lose the ability to effectively coordinate the needs and desires of our spirit, soul (mind, will, emotions), and physical body in harmony with one another. One always overrides leaving the others to be neglected. Either we are so spiritual, or better yet to say—so religious, that we neglect the needs and desires of our body and soul in the name of "serving"

God; sometimes we are too physical, emphasizing the satisfaction of our physical body's needs, wants, and comforts, above doing what we know is the right thing; we are often too emotional, or try to rationalize everything without balancing those emotions or rationalizations against what is going on in us spiritual or physically.

From Hung-over to Hallelujah

The Lord's prescription for the problem was to avoid drinking the product of the grapevine, in any form all together, but that's not all. God never just tells us to stop doing something but He always leads us to what we must do next. It is as the Scripture says in 2 Timothy 2:22,

> "Flee also youthful lusts, but pursue righteousness, faith, love, and peace with all those who call upon the Lord out of a pure heart"

God doesn't just call us from intoxication by sin, but He calls us to purification by His righteousness, faith, love, and peace with those that have a pure heart towards Him. If our efforts are only to stop being trapped into committing certain sins we will never truly be free. The very nature of sin itself predisposes us to continual drunkenness. Sin always takes up multiple residences in our lives; the enemy will come in through the bathroom window, but take up residence in the attic and the living room as well.

Although you may not be actively practicing a given sin any more, and you are effectively avoiding the things that jog the memory of it through that one activity sin can take up residence in other areas of your life. Fornication, for instance, may have been the entry point but your self-esteem and self-image has also been affected. You may have stopped fornicating but the Enemy still has a hold on your self-esteem that He gained through that fornication. Fornication ceases to be the primary point of your intoxication; it is now a negative self-esteem.

We cannot expect to truly be free from sin by attempting to stop one activity when we do we live our life as a former this or that, but never fully as a new creation for whom old things have passed away and all things have become new (2 Cr.5:7) because there is always a residue left over. What's more, we also ought not dwell on our sins or the sins of others because both make us drunk. Deal with sin but dwell on righteousness.

Let's think about this for a moment, if we are not to drink wine what are we to drink then? Well what would a Nazarite have drunk? Water for sure! We know water to be a cleanser, a purifier, and a thirst quencher. Ephesians 5:26 lets us know that it is Jesus who consecrates us and cleanses us by washing us with the water of the word. In the story of the Samaritan woman, Jesus offers her life-satisfying water that would quench her thirst for everything and anything else if she would allow it to spring up into a well of living water in her life (Jhn 4:14-15 & Jhn 7:38). We must drink the water of the word, and the Living Water, the Holy Spirit, and let them begin to purify the entirety of our beings.

In the world there are so many concoctions and potions that people use to sober up and to relieve themselves of the effects of hangovers. In the Kingdom it is water! Water is the key to your sobriety. You may be asking yourself, why am I still struggling, I read the word, I spend time in God's presence, God's Spirit and His word are in my life? The real question you should be asking yourself is am I drinking enough water? The amount of time that you spend in the word and with the Spirit of God ought to be proportionate to the weight of sin whether in thought or deed in your life. It makes sense now why the Scripture says that we should meditate, think on, and speak the word day and night (Joshua 1:8). The more we meditate the more water we drink.

Extra—Above the Ordinary

The freedom that we experience by being washed by the water of His word and being filled with the Living Water, the Holy Spirit is that we gain our senses back and are no longer enslaved by sin or the temptation to sin. Purity reestablishes our wisdom. The Scripture says, "But the wisdom that is from above is first pure" (Jam 3:17). The wisdom that God gives us is birthed out of purity.

We are now able to more accurately interpret the circumstances and situations of our lives from God's perspective by using His wisdom. Christ becomes the power and the wisdom of God in our lives (1 Cor 1:24). With the presence of the Word and of the Holy Spirit in our lives we can expect to be wiser than we have ever been. Not only should we expect an increase in our wisdom, but our memory and imagination should also begin to line up with the greater picture that God has been painting in our lives. The only things that a purified person focuses on from their past are those things that speak to their future. As we remember what the Lord has shown us our future becomes clearer and clearer. If the root of drunkenness was doubt, then the root of sobriety is faith that is built from the wisdom that the Spirit of God deposits into our souls. Just as natural water is filled with minerals so spiritual water is filled with the mineral called faith.

While we were intoxicated by wine we could not coordinate our life's activities in the direction of the extraordinary destiny that we secretly yearned for. With the purification that we receive from the Living Water we can now like never before bring harmony and oneness in the activities of our life. We can see how the success of our spirit will produce the success of our body, which will produce the success of our soul. We can now live our lives with skill because our will and our wisdom are in line with His will and His wisdom. We now begin to live in earnest a life of sobriety. Now that we are sober we can be vigilant, and our adversary the devil can no longer devour us because we will see him for who he is.

I know that you want to live an extraordinary life and do great exploits for your God but before God will use you for the extraordinary you've got to be willing to change what you are drinking. I didn't say you had to be perfect, but you do have to choose your drink more carefully. Drink water–more Spirit-inspired word. The wisdom of the word of God and the presence of the Spirit of God places in your hands the ability to separate, consecrate, and distinguish your inner most being from everything and anything that is in opposition to who you really are in God. In sobriety God grants you the ability to consecrate your inner man for an extraordinary life. Are you willing to make sobriety the order of your life? If sobriety is your lifestyle then God can consecrate you for a lifetime.

Extraordinary Instruction:

1. Consider how you can incorporate more time in the presence of the Lord and meditating in the Word of God into your life.

Journaling the Journey

Consider sharing your thoughts and reflections on www.kimorichardson.com.

CHAPTER 4:

AN EXTRAORDINARY POSITION

"All the days of the vow of his separation there shall no razor come upon his head: until the days be fulfilled, in the which he separateth [himself] unto the LORD, he shall be holy, [and] shall let the locks of the hair of his head grow." *(Numbers 6:5)*

While God is consecrating our inner man He at the same time reveals to us the second dimension of extraordinary living in what He directs the Nazarite to do in conjunction with abstaining from the fruit of the vine. The biblical Nazarite was to make sure that no razor was to touch his hair during the entire time of his consecration to the Lord. At first glance this may seem like a silly instruction but there is much embedded into it in fact it is the natural progression of consecrating the inner man.

The hair on a person's head grows from the nutrients that a person consumes daily; you can tell how well a person eats by the quality of his or her hair. The spiritual application is this, as we begin to consecrate the inner man we naturally grow in to the next dimension of consecration where consecration is not only growing within us but is also growing upon us. Consecration does have an appearance but it is not that of long skirts and doilies, or black suits, collars, and vestments as some have limited it to, it is much more.

A New Look

The Hebrew word that describes the locks of the Nazarite's head reveals the meaning of the instruction that God was giving to Nazarites then and those that would be in the ages to come. The Hebrew root word for hair, sa`ar, gives the word picture of something that is wild or stormy (Blue Letter Bible). The Nazarite was to have an unkempt look about them. They were not to try to manufacture or maintain any semblance of personal grooming where their head was concerned. The Nazarite would be seen by all in this state for the entirety of their consecration. If nothing else this consecration was a trial in humility.

To control a person's appearance is to control the primary mechanism with which they communicate with the world. The unkempt nature of the hair represented the surrendering of the Nazarite's ability to define himself, it represented their rejection of the prepackaged image of success that their present age had to offer, and their reaching for God's definition of who they were to be. This is further confirmed when we examine the Hebrew root word for locks. The Hebrew word pera can also mean leader (Blue Letter Bible). In this second dimension of consecration what was to grow out of the Nazarite was a wild pursuit after God's leadership in their life.

The stormy wildness of their hair was indicative of the wilderness that they were in. A wilderness is anything that is in the state of being wild. The Nazarite's stormy pursuit of God was not to be a momentary reaction but a state of being. It was not to be a private sojourn but a public pursuit for all to see; a pursuit that some would praise and others would scorn.

Look at Moses he is a prime example of this type of pursuit. Moses' pursuit of God was well apparent to all the Israelites; he was a man that had intense favor but at the same time he endured intense scorn even from members of his own family. Moses pursued God in the presence of the Israelites and because of his pursuit every misunderstanding of God that the people had translated into how they treated Moses. This is the price that all Nazarites must be willing to pay. Will you pay the cost of being identified with God? Will you be wild enough to break out of the accepted image of this age and enter the wilderness to pursue God with passion and vigor despite the scorn and misunderstanding of the masses?

A New Place

This is the challenge to those who would be consecrated throughout the ages because true consecration demands a humbling of oneself in what can seem like a very dry and barren place particularly if you are prone to dependency on the opinions of others. With that being said I am not advocating the idea that consecration is about isolation, but I am advocating the idea that it is about exploration.

You must be willing to explore the plan of God for your life as it applies beyond your personal zone of comfort and familiarity, and beyond your expected level of approval from the masses. Again, consecration is simply focused living, living to bring about a desired result, and that result must be more important to you than the approval of the fickle few.

Truth be told though the result that many of us are focusing on right now is not worthy of total life dedication. It is not worthy of the disapproval of the fickle few, which is why we are so tamely pursuing it. Consecrating the way that God requires you to will demand wildness a wildness that drives you into a wilderness experience with the Lord. It will demand a wilderness in which you get so caught up in pursuing God's leadership in your daily life that you lose the neat and tidy 5-year plan that society has carved out for your life. It's not that you don't have a plan but that you are following a plan that is anchored by God's leading.

A Distinguishing Mark

When you pursue God's leadership in your life the same hair that once represented to others the seemingly unkempt and unorganized nature and focus of your life will soon become the distinguishing trademark of your life. You could not miss a Nazarite in

Old Testament Israel when you saw their hair you knew who they were and what they were about. The reward of this dimension of consecration is a clear identity.

One rendering of the Hebrew root word for hair, 'nezer, is crown or mitre, specifically the mitre of the High Priest (Blue Letter Bible). The same hair that represents your wild pursuit of God's leadership will also become your crown. As you pursue God's leadership in your life He crowns you with a grace for leadership and authority. The humility of your pursuit is crowned with a clear identification of who you are in the Kingdom of God and your induction into that priestly office.

According to Exodus 19:6, God has always desired a nation of priests. Though it may seem that you have taken this honor onto yourself in the eyes of the undiscerning because you have humbled yourself in pursuit of God, it is God who crowns you with it.

Your humility legitimizes God's usage of you to represent Him before people and authorizes you to represent people before Him. There are many of us who are stalled in our attempts to take authority over the circumstances that we and others face because we have not been legitimated to represent God to people or to stand before God for people. Understand that it is the grace of God that qualifies you. While it is grace that qualifies you trust and legitimacy are earned consider the parable of the talents in Luke 19 to better understand the pattern of God in this regard. Without the growth of hair upon your head you are not recognized in Heaven or Earth as one who has been crowned with authority by the Lord. Your pursuit is what prepares you for power.

Covering your Consecration

No razor must come upon your head if you really desire to be consecrated. Nothing must stop your pursuit of God's leadership in your life. When that pursuit is stopped you become naked and uncovered. One meaning for the Hebrew word for razor, ``arah, is something which causes you "to pour out" (Blue Letter Bible). The consecration of the inner man will be ruined without the accompanying consecration of the outer man. You can try to live a sober life all you want but if you are unwilling to humble yourself and pursue God with reckless abandon you will never tap into the extraordinary life that you desire.

The humility that God requires is simply that we pursue His leadership with everything that is within us. Humility is not denying who you are and what God has called you to do, but rather it is the acknowledgement of who God has called you to be and your admission that you can never become that without the leadership of an extraordinary God in your life.

That reckless pursuit will undoubtedly lead you into a wilderness experience. Just ask Jesus, John 4 tells us that as soon as He was publicly identified as the Beloved Son of God immediately He was lead into the wilderness by the Spirit of God for an intense season of pursuit and pressure.

The Scripture records that as Jesus sought the Lord with prayer and fasting for the power that He would need to carry out His ministry He was at the same time being tempted of the devil. The devil tried to get Him to doubt that He was who God declared Him to be. Like Jesus each of us will face pressure and a level of persecution as we pursue God's leadership. This pressure comes to make us doubt who we are. As the Old Testament Nazarite was a sight observable to all so the consecrated ones of this day are clearly identifiable and often mocked because of it. I believe when the enemy is looking for someone to attack he searches for hair growing on the head. It is only in the humility of pursuing God's leadership that we are able to withstand the pressure to conform that others will place on us.

The Two Wildernesses

The pressure to conform can itself drive you into a wilderness but this is not the wilderness of consecration it is the wilderness of crisis, one is a wilderness of pursuit the other a wilderness of flight. Flight and pursuit can seem the same because many of the actions that characterize them are the same but the focus is different for each. In flight you are running from, in pursuit you are running to.

The same adrenaline that exhilarates you in pursuit is the same adrenaline that explodes in you when you are in flight. You can be just as busy living in the ordinary as you are in experiencing the extraordinary, just as busy in crisis as you are in consecration. What is so sad about it is that you might never come to know the benefits of being busy in consecration because you are wrapped up in the busyness of attempting to solve various crises. Let's learn more about the wilderness experience so that you can determine which wilderness you are experiencing.

The Hebrew language when referring to the Wilderness of Sinai uses several different words two of which paint very distinct pictures from one another, understanding these words can help us to further understand the duel experiences that can characterize the wilderness experience. The first is "tohu" which means "a desolate unoccupied habitation", it is often expressed in the Scriptures as the Wilderness of Wanderings this is the wilderness of crisis. The second word is "midhbar" which indicates a place that is suitable for pasturing sheep and cattle this is the wilderness of consecration (Dictionary. com). One wilderness is a desolate place that endangers life, the other wilderness is a place that one can be guided to in order to sustain and enrich life. In the wilderness of crisis there is no peace only desolation, but in the wilderness of consecration there is the pastoral leadership of a Supernatural Shepherd who will even make the desert to bloom in order to sustain us as we remain under His care.

No where do we see this concept of the two wildernesses more clearly expressed than in the life of Moses, the man of God. Encoded into Moses from the moment he was born was the destiny to be the deliverer of the Israelites. As it was with Moses so it is with each of us from the moment we are born; God has encoded into us the destiny that He has designed us for but we face the same problem that Moses did we are living among Egyptians. The Scripture indicates that the Egyptians had a distaste for hair, this why Joseph shaved himself before he went into see the Pharaoh (Genesis 41:14).

We are born into a system that discourages wild pursuit after God, a system that never allows us enough time to let the locks of our head grow so that the identity that God has deposited on the inside of our souls can become apparent. Although he was a high-ranking member of the Egyptian system from his youth Moses felt something different stirring inside of him something he could not identify or accurately classify given what he had been trained to pursue and value. His inner frustration caused him to strike out unwisely and kill an Egyptian officer which ultimately caused him to flee into the wilderness of crisis.

Stuck in the Wilderness

There are many people in the body of Christ who are stuck in the wilderness of crisis. In an attempt to be who they think they are and to do what they think is the right thing to do they strike out in quick impulsive actions trying to reach their destiny but are driven further from it. But thanks be to our God who never leaves us stranded but just as He met Moses in his wilderness of crisis so He will meet each one of us. God met Moses in that wilderness and gave him a second chance to be the fullness of who He had designed Him to be and as He did with Moses so He will do for you if you are willing.

I know that you are happy about this second chance that the Lord provides but I want you to notice that God still made Moses go through the wilderness once again because consecration requires a God-ordained wilderness. God did not ordain the wilderness of crisis for you but He will ordain the wilderness of consecration for you.

A New Fire

Moses' wilderness of consecration was not when he took the Israelites to the wilderness but when he entered the wilderness a second time to tend the sheep of Jethro. We know that this was Moses' wilderness of consecration because the Lord declared to Moses when he entered that wilderness that he was on holy ground (Exodus 3:5). Moses located his wilderness of consecration because he was drawn aside by the fire of a burning bush.

A burning bush would not have been a rare sight in the arid wilderness of Sinai, but this bush was different because it burned and was not consumed. This attracted Moses because he realized that if the bush was not being burnt up that the fire that was on it would never dry up. Consecration offers you an eternal fire; every other type of fire will scorch and damage you. Consecration burns every unnecessary thing off of you and enlivens you in a fiery pursuit of the extraordinary.

In Egypt you were set ablaze with lustful, prideful, doubt-filled passions which you pursued with fire and vigor into the wilderness of crisis but the journey of consecration leads you into a different wilderness and sets you ablaze with a different fire. It is in this wilderness that everything that you learned in Egypt must be unlearned, it is in this wilderness that you will see the Lord your God as the fire that must consume your soul, it is in this wilderness that the stormy locks of your head can grow long as you pursue your God and He will crown you with a clear identity in Him.

Extra-Above the Ordinary

When we look at Moses after he entered the wilderness the second time we see a distinct shift in his life. In his wilderness of consecration we see him become a legitimate authority. He could stand before God for the people and be accepted by the Lord. He could represent God before the people even in unbelieving Egypt and see results.

When the Lord would hear none other He heard Moses because he was a recognized authority, when Aaron, Miriam, and Korah lifted their voices against Moses the Lord answered swiftly in judgment leaving no need for Moses to try to defend himself. No one was quite so positioned as Moses because no one understood the purpose for the wilderness experience as much as he did. When the Israelites crossed the Red Sea the wilderness they experienced was supposed to be a wilderness of consecration for all the Israelites but it became a wilderness of crisis because they refused to let the locks of their heads grow, they refused to pursue God in their difficult moments but instead wanted to flee back to Egypt.

Until you can rightly discern the wilderness that you are in you will never achieve true success. Are you wild in pursuing your own passions and tame in pursuing the God that gave you the ability to have those passions? Until you can rightly discern the need to have God as the leader of your life you will never be able to enter your God-ordained destiny. Until you can humble yourself in reckless pursuit of His leadership despite the scorn of others and without being motivated by the praise of others you will never reach true success. Moses spent so much time in the wildness pursuing God that the Scripture records that he was the humblest man on the face of the earth (Numbers 12:3). A clear identification as a God ordained authority is the reward of your pursuit of God. The question you must ask yourself is how bad do I want it? Will you humble yourself in reckless pursuit of Him?

Extraordinary Instruction:
1. Spend sometime in prayer for the next few days and ask the Lord to create in your heart a wild and fiery passion to pursue Him and to reveal and remove everything and anything that seeks to hinder that pursuit.

Journaling the Journey

**Consider sharing your thoughts and reflections
on www.kimorichardson.com.**

CHAPTER 5:

AN EXTRAORDINARY ENVIRONMENT

"All the days that he separateth [himself] unto the LORD he shall come at no dead body. He shall not make himself unclean for his father, or for his mother, for his brother, or for his sister, when they die: because the consecration of his God [is] upon his head...And if any man die very suddenly by him, and he hath defiled the head of his consecration; then he shall shave his head in the day of his cleansing" *(Numbers 6:6-7 + 9)*

As we continue along the journey of consecration the would-be Nazarite is prompted of the Lord to make sure that she keeps herself away from dead bodies and persons that could suddenly die in her presence regardless of how close a relationship she had with them. This instruction seems to be a very strange requirement especially since it prohibits interaction with loved ones at the time when it is most needed for emotional comfort. The Narazite is urged to ignore what seems to be an urgent need in order to fulfill the consecration the she has begun. For all its peculiarity, when we examine this instruction with the eye of the Spirit it proves to be wiser than it seems at face value.

A Work in Progress

The reason that the Nazarite was supposed to stay away from the dead was that the consecrated hair which represented his wild pursuit after the Lord's leadership of his life was still growing. Progress was still being made the consecration was not complete it could still be contaminated if exposed to impurity. In God's instruction to the Nazarite to avoid dead persons we learn how much the environment that one is in can affect the process of consecration. People do affect us the woman and man that seeks to be consecrated must be keenly aware of this.

If most of us were really honest we would willingly admit that we are not as independent as we appear. We are more influenced by our relationships than we willingly acknowledge. Many of us are casting our pearls before swine and ending up with the mud of the pigpen smeared on our lives because of it. There are some people in each of our lives that will not change because of anything we do, nag, or threaten them with. All we can realistically do is leave them alone until they are ready to do what is right before God on their own.

Living in the Graveyard

Truth be told, some of us actually like to keep dead relationships in our lives, not because we intend to help the other person change, but because we refuse to change ourselves. Most of us have been involved in relationships that suffer from some form of dysfunction, as a result of that involvement many of us have unknowingly begun to accept dysfunction as the way that things must be in our lives albeit with some reservation.

Our reservation develops because there is a craving in our hearts that our present relationships cannot satisfy. In order to compensate for our lack of satisfaction many of us attempt to lower our standards for satisfaction. We redefine normal; crisis and dysfunction become normal. We assume that they must be normal because this is what we have seen and experienced in our lives.

This is a moment in which honesty is required. Is this you? Have you tricked yourself into calling pleasurable those activities in your life that are really causing you pain and justifying your experiences by the fact that everyone else you know has gone through it? Have you hidden your own dysfunctions in the deadness of past or present relationships? If you have, then the dead relationships around you have become a cover for your own dysfunction. You have probably even gone so far as to distance yourself from other potential relationships because you have become more comfortable with death and dysfunction than with life and destiny. So long as I am not the only one who can be identified with a

65

dysfunction I'm okay, you say to yourself, but at what price? What is dying in your life because you have chosen to live your life in the graveyard?

You may not have filled your environment with people who are devoid of spiritual life and personal vision, but you allow yourself to entertain relationships with people that have so little life that at any moment they could suddenly drop into some dead work or another. You intentionally surround yourself with people who are not too perfect so that when they fall into a dead work suddenly you can make yourself feel more righteous.

From your holy and righteous position you now become the source of knowledge, prayer, and wisdom. You always have a word of knowledge and a prophecy to give. You always know the right person, or have the finances to bail someone out. You become the source of rescue but not for the other person's sake it is solely to boost your pride. What you need to seriously consider is that if people are suddenly dying around you then it is very possible that there is a plague of sin going around to which you have left yourself susceptible because of your continued association with the dead and dying.

It's an Atmosphere Thing

The Jews understand the need for discernment when it came to dealing with that which is dead; it is a Jewish custom to wash your hands after being in the presence of a dead body whether you have touched them or not (Scheinerman.net). The washing of the hands regardless of whether or not they had touched the person illustrates the fact that the Jews recognize that death affects the atmosphere.

The work of our hands no matter how holy or righteous we perceive it to be is tainted when we abide in the presence of the dead and do not react appropriately. The ordinary person can simply wash his hands and continue on his way, but for the man or woman seeking the extraordinary the stipulation is much more serious. No matter how close a relationship the Nazarite had with an individual if they died in the Nazarite's presence or if the Nazarite went to see them the Nazarite's entire consecration was defiled and she would have to start over again.

The only other persons in Scripture that had such a requirement placed on them were the members of the priesthood. The high priest because of the call of his office was not allowed to even mourn for the dead after all his work was among the living, "let the dead bury their dead" (Matt. 8:22). To the man and woman that would be consecrated their relational environment is of the utmost importance, no matter how sober you get or how humble you become if you do not learn how to sanctify your environment you place your entire consecration at risk.

We still have to be in the world but we do not have to be of the world and it is time that we really reexamine the close relationships that we have and call them what they are. If they are not going up, then they are going down. It is like the Scripture says in the book of Psalms 1 we are blessed when we do not "walk in the counsel of the ungodly, or stand in the path of sinners or sit in the seat of the scornful", however when we follow this thought to its logical conclusion, we understand that we are cursed when we do entertain those types of people in our lives. The person that endeavors to live the consecrated life must carefully consider the impact that the relationships they entertain will have on their environment.

To everything there is a time and a season, if you are in the season of creating an environment around you that will accelerate you into seeing the extraordinary then that which does not agree with the extraordinary must be removed. You must first enter your own wilderness of consecration and abide there before you can return to Egypt and rescue the masses.

How many peoples' goals, dreams, and God-given ambitions do you think have not come to pass because they live in an environment in which the extraordinary is discouraged, not because it is impossible but because it threatens the comfort of those who are around them? It has been said that the richest place on earth is not the oil field but the graveyard. For the one who is seeking the extraordinary embracing dead relationships is tantamount to living in the graveyard.

Even Jesus had to redefine his familial associations when his family members contradicted the workings of God in His life. Jesus asked a crowd of onlookers: Who is my mother? Who is my brother? Who is my sister? He replied that it was those that are doing the will of the Father, those who are alive to the extraordinary, the same rule must apply to you (Matt. 12:50).

Back to Eden: Mastering your Environment

Consecration is not isolation, let me be clear, but it is most definitely a separation from some things unto other things, and from some relationships unto other relationships. Think about it the less time you are spending in dead relationships is the more time that you will spend in relationships in which you are giving and receiving life to the glory of God. The heart of God in leading you to consecrate your environment is not to put you into hiding from the world, but rather to teach you how to master your environment as opposed to having your environment master you. It is only after you learn how to master your environment through deliberately consecrating your environment that you are really able to tackle the fullness of God's assignment for you to go to the sick and become a spring of life.

The vision that God has for your life needs the proper environment in order for it to grow. God has understood the need for the proper environment from the beginning this is the reason that God gave Adam and Eve dominion at the dawn of man's creation. He also understood that dominating your environment is as important as having a sense of purpose. God created the whole earth for man to dominate, but He still saw a need to create on the earth the Garden of Eden as a place where man would learn how to live out being in the image of God which was the purpose for his creation. God loved man so much that He made it a holy place by bringing His presence there day after day.

The first job that man ever had was to maintain his environment (Genesis 2:5). Eden was not the end of man's domain if we read the Genesis text carefully we will discover that man's purpose was to subdue the entire earth. It was God's plan for the entire earth to become man's domain, but nevertheless Adam and Eve had to begin with Eden.

Man had to learn how to subdue anything that would defile Eden. Eden was to be his sacred space. Notice then that it is in Eden that we see how man first defiles his environment. In Genesis 3 we see that rather than subduing the devil man submits to him, and gives him the right to control his domain.

Because he sinned the devil is spiritually dead, "the wages of sin is death" (Rom. 6:23). When man began to entertain conversation with him and to listen to his counsel he in effect went near a dead person, both Adam and Eve entertained relationship with someone that was dead: Eve with the serpent, Adam with Eve. Are you beginning to see how important a consecrated environment is to the completion of your assignment in life? Your purpose is at stake when you do not check the relationships that you entertain and have fellowship with.

Distinguishing the Dead

As a point of clarification, do not assume that the only dead people are those that are not saved, because in some respects some unsaved people are more alive than those who do the religious thing on a consistent basis. Jesus was called a friend of prostitutes and drunkards among other things, but the Scriptures also make the interesting statement that it was those prostitutes and sinners who would enter

Heaven before some the religious people of Jesus' day (Luke 7:34).

To be clear, your closest relationships should be with those who are filled with the Spirit—those who live in relationship with God, and you should always seek counsel from the godly, but unsaved people should be in your domain, these are the people that God will release us to reach for the Kingdom as we grow consecrated in our environment. You need an environment of those that are truly seeking the extraordinary and sometimes you have to leave the comfort of familiar relationships in order to find that.

If there was one area in which Samson continually failed it was this one. He constantly entertained relationships with Philistine women, yet these were the very ones he was raised up to deliver Israel from. Israel never experienced that deliverance due to his dabbling with the dead. What have you not accomplished because you continue to dabble with the dead?

We must also separate those relationships that are truly dead ones from those relationships in which you are simply annoyed with the person. You need to forgive them. Realize that relationships are critical in both harming and building our life's destiny so ask the Lord to lead you in identifying dead relationships as opposed to those relationships that are simply in need of repair. If your brother has sinned against you tell him his fault, forgive him, and win him back if he is willing (Matt 18).

Extra-Above the Ordinary

The sacrifice of sanctity is to separate yourself from relationships that have become familiar to you when they become deadly to you. As it was said before real consecration is simply a re-emphasis of the most fundamental elements of dedicated living, and not everyone will be as dedicated to change as you will. The reward of sanctifying your environment is that you free yourself from being plagued by the crises of others long enough to discover your Eden, that sphere in which God has declared that you have been given dominance in. In Eden death does not dictate to you but you dictate to it.

Once you find Eden you are given a choice that you have not had before, a choice that man failed to make the first time he was in Eden; you get to choose the tree of life—the tree of possibility and potential. So long as you entertain dead relationships you don't have this choice nor can you really help those that need your help. Will you sanctify your environment by sanctifying your relationships? Sanctification is the key to your elevation.

Extraordinary Instruction:

1. Ask the Lord to identify dead relationships around you and to give you the strength to separate from those relationships and help you to sanctify your environment.

Journaling the Journey

Consider sharing your thoughts and reflections on www.kimorichardson.com.

CHAPTER 6:

THE FULLNESS OF CONSECRATION

"And this [is] the law of the Nazarite, when the days of his separation are fulfilled"
Numbers 6:13

So many times when we engage in spiritual disciplines there seems to be no net result from the activity other than our having done it. But thank God at the end of consecration there are tangible results that can be expected. There is fullness in consecration, a point at which we tip the scales and begin to achieve that for which we have sought God.

Remember that I said in the beginning that when we consecrate for the extraordinary we consecrate with the specific end in mind of being able to offer to God an acceptable offering. The Scripture admonishes us that we should do everything as though we are doing it for the Lord, so even if the area that you need to see the extraordinary in is not a particularly spiritual one don't worry it is still acceptable.

I don't think that we understand the power of having an acceptable offering to give to God; Giving an acceptable offering means that we have come to possess that which we have offered and can continue to possess it in the fullness. As we consider that which the Nazarite was able to offer we gain a picture of that which we become full of in consecration.

Full of Firsts

The first thing that the Nazarite was able to offer was a male lamb in its first year without blemish as a burnt offering to the Lord. To the modern day Nazarite the male lamb represents the entirety of his life. The first thing that God wants to receive as an offering from you is not your money or your part of your time, but rather your identity. He wants you to offer yourself to Him to the point that you die to selfish goals and ambitions. He wants you to live your life as a living sacrifice totally devoted to worshipping Him with the entirety of your being.

You were never able to offer yourself to God like that before, even when you wanted to give your life over to God completely so that you could live in the extraordinary you would always discover a fault or a blemish that would prohibit you from giving yourself to God completely for fear of rejection. You would bring yourself before the priests—your parents, your boss, your pastor to offer yourself but you were rejected because everyone noticed your blemish, but now that you have allowed God the opportunity to consecrate that which is within you, around you, and upon you, you can now give God your life as an acceptable offering dedicated to His plan and glory in the world. Being this type of offering illustrates the fact that you have abandoned trying to worship God through your own merit, and you have conformed yourself to the pattern of Christ, because every burnt offering was a reminder to God of the sacrifice that His Son would give. You remind God of Jesus at this level of consecration.

This offering that the Nazarite gave was no trivial thing not only was the Nazarite offering something unique to God, but the Nazarite was offering it in an unprecedented way. The male lamb was to be a lamb in its first year. It was God's command to the people of Israel that the first of everything was to be offered to God with the understanding that the first represents and sanctifies everything else (Deut. 18:4).

To be able to offer yourself as a firstfruit signifies the kind of change that has occurred in the life of the offerer. As the firstfruit you become the trendsetter and the example, the first in the lineage. You become the example of the extraordinary you want to see. The crisis that once dominated and defined your identity no longer defines you, you now define it. You share in Jesus' identity as the first among many brethren (Rom. 8:29). You become the first to overcome with the ability to help others to achieve what you have achieved. You become filled with the ability to produce firsts.

Full Confidence

The second thing that the Nazarite was to offer was a female lamb in the first year which was to represent the sin offering. Sin in the life of a man or woman that is striving to achieve righteousness is the most debilitating thing that they have to face, you ever been there? Praying and seeking God with intensity and vigor, doing what you know is right but then out of no where it seems that sin is crouched at your door desiring to overtake you. Sin is a confidence breaker, and when your confidence is broken so also is your strength.

God knows that seeking the extraordinary does not mean that we are immune to the attack of temptation, nor does it mean that we will not sin, so he instructs the Nazarite to offer a perpetual offering for sin. Why do I call it a perpetual offering? I call it a perpetual offering not because the Nazarite would never have to offer another sacrifice for sin again, but because this offering was a reminder to the Nazarite that there was always an offering for sin that could be offered, there was always hope and redemption.

Sometimes we can get so high, so far, so deep in God that when we sin or are close to it there seems to be no more remedy for it. Who can we tell? Where can we go? How can we be helped? There yet remains a remedy for sin, the remedy is Christ. Consecration is not perfection it is simply focus, focus on the goal of apprehending that for which Christ has apprehended us (Phl. 3:12).

As we pursue the extraordinary we are not to cast away our confidence, but rather to base our confidence not on how wonderful we are or how great we have become but rather on Christ. The female lamb is to compliment the male lamb; the only way that we will ever really be able to perpetually offer ourselves as a living sacrifice is to recognize that there is one perpetual sacrifice that is always available if we fall it is in this sacrifice that we must trust. We can trust this sacrifice not only because it is available if we fall, but it can keep us from falling. We experience a fullness of confidence even when we make mistakes because we know there yet remains a sacrifice for sin of which we can partake.

Full Relationship

Not only can we trust that the Lord will forgive sin and restore our confidence but we can now experience a fullness of relationship with Him. The Nazarite was also to offer a ram without blemish and that was to be a peace offering, an offering of fellowship between God and man. There is another level of fellowship that is afforded to the man or woman that consecrates themself.

The Scriptures teach us that it is in God we live, in God we move, and in God we have our very being, but few of us ever really experience a relationship with God that approximates anything like that (Acts 17:28). We are always on earth appealing to Heaven, always at the door knocking, seeking admission into Kingdom affairs. We've had to be on the outside before because we never really took the time to understand God's objectives even for our own lives.

The Nazarite was instructed to take his consecrated hair which resented his pursuit of God and put it under the fire of the peace offering symbolizing the fact that his fellowship with God is fueled by his pursuit of God. As we pursue God in consecration we are offered the opportunity to tap into the heart of God, the hope of God, and the hand of God. We don't move without Him, and He doesn't move without us.

Before consecration we were rams that pushed and shoved our way into what we wanted and away from where God was leading we now become rams that push those things that impede our fellowship with God out of our way. And not only do we remove those things that impede our fellowship with God, but we also remove those things that impede our fellowship with other men and women who have been crowned with authority by the Lord. The peace offering was brought to the priest and became his wave offering which symbolized the Nazarite's fellowship with the priest and expressed honor for him (Num. 6:19-20).

A Full Mouth

We are to offer all of these things with unleavened bread mingled with oil. Bread in the Scriptures has been used to represent words, and oil has been used as a symbol for the anointing of the Holy Spirit. The offering of bread mixed with oil signifies the fact that we now begin to utter words that are mingled with the anointing of the Holy Spirit. In the making of bread oil helps to flavor bread and helps the dough to combine. The oil of the anointing gives your words

79

the ability to stick and have effect. You now abide in Him and His word in you and you can ask what you will because you do not ask amiss any more and you will have it (Jhn. 15:7).

A Full Hand

As we offer all of this to the Lord, God now brings us to the place that we have been pressing and seeking for the fullness of consecration. The fullness of consecration is not a look, or a dress, it is not attendance at religious functions or anything of that sort. The Scriptures record that the priest would take the peace offering and place it in the hands of the Nazarite.

When the Bible says that the priest would place the ram in the hands of the Nazarite the Hebrew expression, "fill the hand," means to consecrate (Blue Letter Bible). Consecration in its fullness supplies your hands with a work to do, and not only a work to do but the means to do it. When you truly consecrate something you fill it so that there is not room for anything else. In consecration purpose is revealed and provision is provided to accomplish the will of God for our lives.

A Fullness of the Spirit

The final thing that God declares to the Nazarite at the end of his consecration is that he can now consume wine again. Although the Nazarite was to consume wine again I do not think that it is the same wine, in other words this is not permission for the

Nazarite to engage in sin once again, this wine represents the Holy Spirit.

In the Gospels Jesus references what He calls new wine, this wine is representative of the newness of life that comes when the Holy Spirit fills our lives (Luk. 5:37). During our consecration we have been filling ourselves with the water of the word which has been purifying and cleansing us. As we reach the fullness of consecration I believe that a transformation occurs.

Just as Jesus turned the water into wine at the wedding at Cana, so He transforms the Living Water into the Filling Wine that empowers our lives.

So many of us yearn to know the Holy Spirit as One who empowers and delivers, but we must first know Him as One who purifies. We must become new wineskins that are able to handle the new wine. When this wine comes it causes us to grow, expand, and develop beyond our own capacity and according to His capacity within us. We become full of His ability to accomplish that which we have vowed to Him, we now have the power to do what is necessary and to receive results.

The Fullness of Consecration

As we experience the fullness of consecration in all these ways we can begin to engage the world with skill and with success and see the extraordinary hand of God in our lives. There are some works that will be established right away, and for others we will have to be like the generals of faith who began to reach for goals so big and so great that it would take more than one generation to see those things accomplished, but they yet held on to the promise that they had received knowing that they would have those things for which they sought; Great things, Glorious things, Extraordinary things! Will you strive for the fullness of consecration?

Journaling the Journey

**Consider sharing your thoughts and reflections
on www.kimorichardson.com.**

THE MOST EXTRAORDINARY INSTRUCTION

To be honest with you after I had written the previous chapter I thought that I was done with this book, it was only after having watched one of my favorite preachers that I realized that this last section of this book could not go unwritten because it is truly the icing on the cake. Hopefully you have reached this section of the book having gained the understanding that reaching the extraordinary is a legal process that affects what is within us, upon us, and around us. While it is a legal process it is not a mechanical one it is personal, God gets involved in the process and challenges you to know Him and His ways in greater detail.

To truly know God is to love Him with "all your heart, with all your mind, with all your soul, and with all your strength". In fact the law of the extraordinary wouldn't work if you don't hang it on the greatest law of all which is to love God with everything that is within you, upon you, and around you. Jesus said that every other law found in the Scriptures hangs upon the law of loving God with everything and loving your neighbor as yourself (Matt. 22:37-40).

Sobriety, humility, and sanctity will only fill you with a sense of pride and religiosity if they are not powered by a burgeoning desire to love God more and to have an extraordinary impact on the people in your sphere of influence. Remember that God has power, but He is love. Love is the One who empowers the surpassing and mighty works you desire.

Beyond any instruction that I could write within this book to assist you along your journey God has given the most extraordinary instruction that can ever be given; Love God and others with intensity and vigor so that God's love can power your every action. So if you are looking for the great, the extraordinary, the immeasurable works of God in your life continue to let the love of God be the guide for all your actions. This is what you do when the ordinary won't do!

Journaling the Journey

Consider sharing your thoughts and reflections on www.kimorichardson.com.

BIBLIOGRPHY

Chapter 1:
Blue Letter Bible. "Dictionary and Word Search for *'naziyr (Strong's 05139)'* " . Blue Letter Bible. 1996-2002. 10 Nov 2006. <http://www.blueletter-bible.org/cgi-bin/words.pl?word=05139&page=1>

Blue Letter Bible. "Dictionary and Word Search for *'pala' (Strong's 06381)'* " . *Blue Letter Bible.* 1996-2002. 18 Oct 2006. <http://www.blueletter-bible.org/cgi-bin/words.pl?word=06381&page=1>

Chapter 3:
Blue Letter Bible. "Dictionary and Word Search for *'yada` (Strong's 03045)'* " . *Blue Letter Bible.* 1996-2002. 19 Oct 2006. <http://www.blueletter-bible.org/cgi-bin/words.pl?word=03045&page=1>

"Effects of Alcohol Intoxication." *Indiana.edu.* 1 Nov 2006. http://www.indiana.edu/~adic/effects.html

Chapter 4:

Blue Letter Bible. "Dictionary and Word Search for *'sa`ar (Strong's 08175)'* ". *Blue Letter Bible.* 1996-2002. 19 Oct 2006. <http://www.blueletter-bible.org/cgi-bin/words.pl?word=08175&page=1>

Blue Letter Bible. "Dictionary and Word Search for *'pera` (Strong's 06545)'* ". *Blue Letter Bible.* 1996-2002. 19 Oct 2006. <http://www.blueletter-bible.org/cgi-bin/words.pl?word=06545&page=1>

Blue Letter Bible. "Dictionary and Word Search for *'nezer (Strong's 05145)'* ". *Blue Letter Bible.* 1996-2002. 19 Oct 2006. <http://www.blueletter-bible.org/cgi-bin/words.pl?word=05145&page=1>

Blue Letter Bible. "Dictionary and Word Search for *'`arah (Strong's 06168)'* ". *Blue Letter Bible.* 1996-2002. 19 Oct 2006. <http://www.blueletter-bible.org/cgi-bin/words.pl?word=06168&page=1>

Dictionary.com. "wilderness." *Easton's 1897 Bible Dictionary.* 19 Oct. 2006. <Dictionary.com http://dictionary.reference.com/browse/wilderness>

Chapter 5:

Scheinerman.net. "The Jewish Life Cycle: Death." *Scheinerman.net.* 1 Nov 2006. http://scheinerman. net/judaism/life-cycle/death.html

Chapter 6:

Blue Letter Bible. "Dictionary and Word Search for *'male' (Strong's 04390)'* " . Blue Letter Bible. 1996-2002. 2 Nov 2006. <http://www.blueletter-bible.org/cgi-bin/words.pl?word=04390&page=1>

ABOUT THE AUTHOR

L.A. Kimo Richardson is a minister at the Abundant Life Family Worship Church in New Brunswick New Jersey. In addition to being an author, he is also the C.E.O. of Aspiring Eloquence, a communication coaching company that specializes in helping individuals to achieve "eloquence in every expression".

To contact the author and to learn about how you can start a relationship with God log on to:

www.kimorichardson.com

Printed in the United States
74086LV00001B/29

9 781602 660625